The Life and Times of

Saint John Boste

Catholic Martyr

of Durham

1544-1594

Simon Webb

The author is a Member of Northumbria Area Meeting of the Religious Society of Friends (Quakers)

Spelling, punctuation and use of capitals have been modernised in quotations from Elizabethan sources. Explanations of some words follow them in square brackets.

To my friend, Sean Matthew Smith

## Also From the Langley Press

In Search of the Northern Saints

A Little Book of English Saints

In Search of the Celtic Saints

Bede's Life of Saint Cuthbert

The Legend of St Cuthbert

Gilbert's Tale: The Life and Death of Thomas Becket

For free downloads and more from the Langley Press, please visit
our website at http://tinyurl.com/lpdirect

# Contents

# 1. A Golden Age?

If you believe that the reign of Queen Elizabeth I was a golden age in English history, you might want to express your belief with caution when you find yourself in the company of a descendant of one of the grand old Roman Catholic families of Britain. Like many other alleged golden ages, including the 1950s in the United States, and the Edo period in Japan, the Elizabethan age may have been golden for some, but for others it was merely thinly gilded. For many English Catholics, there was no gilding at all: the age had the harshness of steel and the poisonous quality of lead.

True, the age of 'Gloriana' had its 'golden lads and girls', to borrow a phrase from Shakespeare. Among these was Shakespeare himself, of course, and his fellow-playwrights Christopher Marlowe and Ben Jonson: all three managed to be superb poets as well as playwrights. Also among the poets were Edmund Spenser and Sir Philip Sidney, the latter a true aristocratic English renaissance man, who also wrote in prose, and may have been the first truly significant writer in English since the fourteenth century, and Geoffrey Chaucer. As well as writing, Sidney was a gifted linguist in both living and dead languages. He was also very well-travelled, met many notable people, and worked as a distinguished diplomat, soldier and courtier. Shakespeare, who borrowed ideas from him, may have been thinking of someone like the handsome, well-dressed Sidney when he had Ophelia describe Hamlet as:

The courtier's, soldier's, scholar's, eye, tongue, sword,
Th' expectancy and rose of the fair state,
The glass of fashion and the mould of form,
Th' observed of all observers . . .

Although at times Sidney's Elizabethan world must have appeared to him to be a succession of fine feasts, dances, intellectual discussions, engaging books and fittings for gorgeous outfits, he had also seen the darker side of life in Europe in the later sixteenth century.

He had been in Paris at the time of the St Bartholomew's Day Massacre of August 1572, and no doubt watched, horrified, from the windows of the English embassy while bands of French Catholics killed hundreds of their fellow-countrymen because they were, like Sidney, Protestants.

At home, Philip knew of, but is thought not to have approved of, the persecution of Roman Catholics, though he was involved in drafting punitive laws against them, and derived part of his income from monies seized from the so-called 'recusants'. These were people who refused to attend the Protestant services of the Tudor state church, and who incurred fines, and far worse punishments, as a result. As if to demonstrate how much power the secular aristocracy of England had over the state church at the time, Sidney also derived some of his income from money that should have been used to support Church of England priests.

Among the men Sidney spoke with on his travels was Edmund Campion, whom he might also have met years earlier back in England. Philip may have been present at Oxford in 1566, when that city was visited in triumphant style by Queen Elizabeth. Sidney would have been a precocious and promising twelve year-old at the time: at twenty-six, Campion was already a fellow of the then very new St John's College, which had been founded in Queen Mary's time. The future martyr and saint was a much sought-after tutor and lecturer, and 'the glass of fashion and the mould of form' for the younger scholars, who even tried to imitate his deep, compelling voice and his way of walking.

Like shop-keepers putting their best wares in the windows of their shops, the university fielded Campion to give a speech of welcome to Queen Elizabeth at the start of her 1566 visit. He also participated in a debate set up to be watched by the queen during her time in Oxford. Despite his comparative youth, Campion was already an old hand at this sort of thing. Eight years earlier, in his home town of London, Edmund had been chosen to give an address to Elizabeth's half-sister, the Catholic Queen Mary, as she rode through London on the way to her coronation.

Campion's youthful success was even more remarkable because his antecedents were far more humble than Philip Sidney's. The son of a bookseller, Edmund had relied on grants (then called 'exhibitions') from the Grocers' Company in London to get him to university in the first place, and later to further his career in the state church.

Although there were many meatier issues that Campion and his fellow participants in the show-debate at Oxford could have chewed over, in the end they entertained Elizabeth with a discussion about what caused the tides to go in and out. Among other more pressing issues at the time were the legitimacy or otherwise of Elizabeth's status as queen, and the wisdom or otherwise of the state's abandonment of Mary's Roman Catholic religion on Elizabeth's succession.

In terms of worldly success, the best thing that could happen to a promising young scholar in Campion's position in those days was to gain the patronage of a representative of one of the wealthy aristocratic families that wielded so much power in Elizabethan times. Even Philip Sidney, for all his aristocratic background, relied on patrons, since his family was not as rich as its grand titles might have suggested. Later Sidney allied himself to even more power by marrying the daughter of Queen Elizabeth's spy-master, Sir Francis Walsingham, of whom more later. Sidney's new father in-law agreed to underwrite a huge chunk of Philip's debts, equalling over a quarter of a million pounds in today's money.

On the strength of his performances before the queen at Oxford in the summer of 1566, Edmund Campion caught the eye of Robert Dudley, the famous Earl of Leicester who became a long-standing favourite of the queen. A widower in 1566, Leicester was even tipped as a possible future husband for Elizabeth: a man with an eye for talent, like Elizabeth herself, he also acted as a patron to his nephew, Philip Sidney.

Edmund Campion received his second Grocers' Company exhibition in the month after his great success in front of the queen at Oxford, and this led to his being ordained a deacon in 1569 – a position that also had a useful income attached to it.

But, if he had ever been truly attracted to it, Campion was now losing interest in the successful future career that was evidently waiting for him in the state church. He could no longer hide or otherwise mitigate his growing devotion to the old religion, and in 1571 he broke the law by leaving England without a passport and travelling to the English Catholic college at Douai, then in Flanders.

The English College at Douai existed thanks to the efforts of William Allen, a remarkable man from Lancashire. Like Campion a graduate of Oxford, and once an important man at the university, Allen's academic career in England collapsed when the Protestant Elizabeth mounted the throne. After some time in the Low Countries, Allen returned to his native Lancashire and was shocked to see how far his fellow-Catholics had compromised with the new religion. Leaving England for the last time in 1565, in 1568 he founded the new English College at the University of Douai, which itself had only been in existence since 1559.

At first, conditions in the 'large house and very convenient' that the college rented were spartan, but as Allen assembled more sources of income, more students and more prestige for himself and his new foundation, Douai became a sort of headquarters for exiled English Catholics, whether priests or lay people.

Edmund Campion's arrival at Douai in 1571 constituted the placing of a large metaphorical feather in the cap of Allen's college; but between 1573 and 1580 Edmund was teaching in Moravia and Bohemia. It was in Bohemia, in the city of Prague, that Philip Sidney conversed with Campion in 1576: by this time Campion was a Jesuit.

William Allen wrote a letter to Campion in 1579, calling him to

Rome. His purpose was to send Edmund with a small party of like-minded colleagues back to England, to help in the effort to re-convert England to the old religion, or at least to give succour to the Catholics who had been left high and dry by the legal restrictions on Catholicism. Cuthbert Mayne, who knew Campion and was another alumnus of both Oxford and Douai, had become the first of William Allen's so-called 'seminary priests' to be martyred at the hands of the English authorities, in Cornwall in 1577. A Devon man himself, Mayne bore the name of Durham's favourite saint simply because he had been baptised on St Cuthbert's day – March the twentieth.

Mayne had posed as a steward working for a Cornish magnate, and Campion adopted the alias of a trader in jewels from Dublin. The latter travelled around the country, staying with prominent Catholic families, ministering to them as a priest, writing and having his writings published clandestinely. Meanwhile in January 1581 a proclamation instructed the authorities to arrest any Jesuits discovered in England; and a new law defined any attempt to turn Protestant English people back to 'the Romish religion' as treason.

At last, Campion and nine others were apprehended at the house of a sympathiser called Edward Yates at his home, Lyford Grange in Berkshire. They had been betrayed by one George Eliot, a Catholic turned informer. Eliot helped search the house, a procedure which involved knocking on walls and panelling and breaking down or ripping out anything that sounded hollow. By nightfall, two of the fugitives had been found hiding in a dovecot; but where were the rest? It was not until the next morning that one of the searchers noticed a chink of light above the stairs, and took a crow-bar to it. The priests were found inside, lying on a bed, surrounded by provisions for three or four days.

The prisoners were taken to London. On the journey, they were treated well at first, but at the Berkshire village of Colnbrook their hands were tied and they were also tied onto their horses. A sign saying 'THE SEDITIOUS JESUIT' was fastened to Campion's hat.

At the Tower of London, Campion was placed for a while in a tiny cell called 'Little Ease' in which it was impossible for a man of average height and girth to either lie down or stand up. There were similar cells in other prisons around the country at the time.

Among Campion's papers that had been published during his stay in England was one, often called *Campion's Brag*, that challenged Protestant churchmen and others to participate in public disputes with him, 'wherein I undertake to avow the faith of our Catholic Church by proofs innumerable, scriptures, councils, fathers, history, natural and moral reasons'.

In the Tower, the Jesuit was given the opportunity to dispute during four sessions held there in August and September 1581; but these had been set up in such a way that Campion was severely disadvantaged. The deans and distinguished theologians who were lined up against him on chairs not only outnumbered him – they also had access to numerous books and notes, and were allowed to make their own notes. The Jesuit, seated on a stool, had only the Bible, was not allowed pen and ink, and had been given only a few hours to prepare: we may be sure that his opponents had spent many hours preparing, both together and alone. The Protestant side dictated the subjects to be discussed in the Tower debates, and also laid down the rules of the debates, which often dictated that Campion should remain silent. Worse, Campion had by now been subjected to hours of stretching on the rack, and other tortures, and his health was utterly broken and his memory defective. Nevertheless, although he made a few mistakes, the Catholics who were present felt that he had done well, and the authorities responded by publishing a version of events that cut out much of what Campion had said.

After some changes made to the charges against him, Campion and some of his fellow-prisoners were subjected to what amounted to a shameful show-trial, where they were found guilty of having been part of a Europe-wide conspiracy to kill the queen, invade England and enforce Catholicism. Edmund Campion was hanged, drawn and quartered at Tyburn in London on the first day of December 1581.

## 2. A Reign of Terror

In his biography of William Shakespeare, the novelist Anthony Burgess came close to describing the grisly business of hanging, drawing and quartering condemned men as the supreme expression of the hangman's art, in keeping with the edgy creativity of the Elizabethan and Jacobean ages. The practice is the reason why Shakespeare's Macbeth remarks on his blood-stained 'hangman's hands': this has been known to confuse modern readers and play-goers, who think that bloodshed was not a feature of hanging during its last days as part of the justice system in England. Then, the ideal was to kill the prisoner instantly, but without beheading him: this was done behind closed doors, in the presence of a few witnesses. The sentence of hanging, drawing and quartering as used during Elizabeth's reign was designed to prolong the agony and bloodshed, and often to maximise the spectacle for the benefit of the thousands of members of the public who could turn up for these events, regarding them as free entertainment.

In those days, and for a long time after in England, hanging often meant slow strangulation, not the neck-snapping 'long drop' of the twentieth-century British hangman. Friends and relatives of the victim would often pull on his legs to shorten the agony, but in theory, during the more elaborate procedure of hanging, drawing and quartering, the victim was cut down while he was still conscious. His heart would then be pulled out and shown to him, it and his other entrails and his genitals would be flung into boiling water and, at last, the body would be cut up into four quarters. These, as well as the head, were often put on display as a warning to others who might be thinking of offending. In London the fourth part, the head, would also be put on show on London Bridge: to prevent its being eaten in a matter of minutes by the city's seagulls, the head would first be prepared by parboiling it with salt and cumin.

It seems that, mercifully, Edmund Campion was already dead, or at least unconscious, when they cut him down. In the case of the martyr William Hart, the crowd that had assembled to watch his hanging, drawing and quartering at York in May 1583 took pity on the victim and intervened, fending off the hangman until Hart was well and truly dead at the end of the rope. There is a link between Hart and John Boste, the subject of this little biography: an essay by Hart was found at the home of Boste's brother Lancelot when government agents were questioning him about John's whereabouts in 1583. Lancelot insisted that the essay had nothing to do with him, but must have been left behind by his brother.

The plight of a Durham martyr called Joseph Lambton, a descendant of the Sir John Lambton who had killed the local dragon known as the Lambton Worm, provoked the pity not just of the spectators but of the hangman himself. This functionary became so overwhelmed by the horror of what he was doing to Father Lambton that he abandoned the process while the victim was still conscious and only partially dismembered. A local butcher had to be called in to finish the work: this was in Newcastle in 1593, the year before the martyrdom of John Boste.

In the case of Edward Waterson, a Londoner who was martyred at Newcastle in the same year as Lambton, the horses that were supposed to drag him to the gallows flatly refused to do so, even when they were replaced by a second team. In the end, Waterson had to walk to the gallows. There, he found that the ladder he was supposed to climb up to get to the top of the gallows was shaking uncontrollably: he stilled it by making the Sign of the Cross.

Shocking as it was, the sentence carried out in the case of Edmund Campion was neither as prolonged nor as agonising as that passed on Margaret Clitherow, a Catholic housewife of York, five years later. Margaret, who was about thirty years old at the time, was tried for the crime of harbouring Catholic priests, but refused to plead either guilty or not guilty, saying 'I know no offence whereof I should confess myself guilty'. She was sentenced to be stripped naked and forced to lie under heavy weights for three days without food or water. On the third day, it was proposed that she should be finally pressed to death. In the event, Margaret's tormentors took pity on her and pressed her to death in the course of fifteen minutes, instead of three days. She was declared a saint in 1929, and a house in the old York street called The Shambles, where she used to live, is now kept as a shrine to her memory.

Margaret Clitherow's sentence, known as *peine fort et dure*, had been introduced in the fourteenth century to punish people who, like her, would plead neither guilty or not guilty. But those who watched her being crushed to death – a procedure that made her ribs burst right out of her skin – knew perfectly well that Margaret was really being punished for her adherence to the Roman Catholic faith. This was also the case for Edmund Campion and the many other martyrs who were hanged, drawn and quartered under Queen Elizabeth, though their particular type of execution was supposed to have been designed for traitors.

The reason why Campion, Boste and the others were regarded as traitors goes to the heart of the relationship between the Protestant English state under Elizabeth and the Roman Catholic religion. This relationship was part of what made Elizabeth's time on the throne a reign of terror, though the terror was experienced on both sides of the religious divide.

We have already seen how Philip Sidney witnessed the massacre of Protestants by Catholics in Paris in 1572 from the safety of the city's English embassy. Although Shakespeare's contemporary, the aforementioned playwright and poet Christopher Marlowe, wrote a play about this event called *The Massacre at Paris*, the massacre itself spread far beyond the French capital, and many thousands were killed. The fear that something similar might happen in England was exacerbated by the fact that three years earlier, in 1569, there was a

Catholic-inspired rebellion in the north of England, called variously 'the Earls' Rebellion', 'the Rising in the North', 'the Revolt of the Northern Earls' or 'the Northern Rebellion'.

In November 1569 the Catholic rebels entered Durham cathedral and destroyed the Protestant prayer-books; and Thomas Plumtree, who was made a saint in 1986, celebrated the Catholic Mass. The rebels also occupied nearby Barnard Castle and the port of Hartlepool, and marched south as far as Bramham Moor in Yorkshire. Elizabeth responded to this threat with a large military force: the rebels retreated back north and some six hundred people connected to the rebellion were killed.

A similar Catholic rebellion against the new Protestant order had taken place over thirty years earlier, in 1536, during the reign of Elizabeth's father, King Henry VIII. This was the Pilgrimage of Grace, during which the rebels managed to seize the important city of York, Margaret Clitherow's home town; but this rebellion also ended with hundreds of rebels being killed by order of the Tudor monarch.

Between the Pilgrimage of Grace and the rebellion of 1569 there had been the reign of Elizabeth's Catholic half-sister Queen Mary, who ruled from 1553 to 1558. She attempted to restore her kingdom to Catholicism, an attempt that was enthusiastically supported by the aforementioned William Allen, who rose to prominence in England at this time, becoming principal of St Mary Hall, Oxford. The so-called 'Marian persecutions' saw hundreds of Protestants killed for their faith, many of them being burned at the stake.

As if all this wasn't enough to make Elizabeth's Protestant regime nervous of the country's Catholics, in 1570, the year after the northern rebellion, Pope Pius V issued a papal bull declaring the excommunication of Elizabeth I.

Papal bulls were so called because of the lead seals or 'bulla' that were attached to them. Historians tend to identify them by the first words of the document proper, and Pius's bull of the twenty-fifth of February 1570 was called *Regnans in Excelsis* ('reigning on high' in

Latin). The text of the bull opened with the assertion that 'He who reigns on high' had laid down that there could only ever be one true church, which He had entrusted to the apostle St Peter. Roman Catholic popes regard themselves as Peter's heirs, and in *Regnans in Excelsis* Pius claimed that this gave him the right to rule over all the kingdoms of the world.

After asserting Pius's authority, *Regnans in Excelsis* goes on to lament the growth in the numbers of the ungodly, an increase that Elizabeth, 'pretended queen of England and the servant of crime' actively encouraged, giving sanctuary to pernicious people. Elizabeth had ruined her country by suppressing the true religion, and had replaced Catholic noblemen on the royal council with heretical commoners.

Despite Elizabeth's godly ancestors, Pius states that he feels obliged to excommunicate the queen and her supporters, cutting her off from Christ. The bull goes on to declare that Elizabeth no longer has any right to call herself queen, and that anyone who obeys her commands should also consider themselves to be excommunicated.

In his bull *Regnans in Excelsis* Pope Pius expressed his contempt for the idea that Elizabeth claimed to be the head of the English Church, thus usurping what he regarded as his own role. The British monarch's supremacy over the Anglican Church is still asserted, of course, and the abbreviation 'fid. def.' (for the Latin *fidei defensatrix*) that is to be found on British coins denotes 'defender of the faith'. This dignity was first claimed by Elizabeth's father King Henry VIII, and then and now it was controversial among Roman Catholics and some Protestants. Nicholas Harpsfield, a Roman Catholic priest and biographer of Thomas More who suffered persecution under Elizabeth, wrote that:

albeit the Grecians long ago abandoned the See of Rome, and of late the Germans, yet were they never so bad or mad as to attribute the said supremacy to any lay prince . . .

Harpsfield's mention of the 'Grecians' refers to the split between what is now called the Eastern Orthodox Church and the Latin Church of the west, which occurred in 1054.

Among some Protestant commentators, both now and in Elizabethan times, there was and is a feeling that the English Church was never thoroughly reformed, as the Church was elsewhere in Europe. Did Elizabeth's father Henry VIII merely create a miniature national version of the Roman Catholic Church, casting himself as a new local type of pope? The fact that, then as now, the Church of England retained bishops and archbishops (which were, however, abolished for a brief period during the Interregnum) has suggested to some that this was indeed the case.

The idea that Elizabeth had no real right to the English throne, which is expressed in Pius's bull, was supported by many Catholics on the grounds that she was the daughter of Henry VIII's second wife, Anne Boleyn. The story of Henry's divorce from his first wife, the Spanish princess Katherine of Aragon, and his marriage to Anne, is of course one of the most famous tales from English history. The fact that the pope of the time would not allow the divorce was one of the reasons Henry turned his back on Rome and embraced the new reformed religion of Luther and 'the Germans' mentioned by Nicholas Harpsfield.

Since it had not approved it, the Catholic Church did not accept the validity of Henry's divorce from Katherine. This made Anne Boleyn not Henry's second wife, at least in their eyes, but at best his concubine; so that any children of their union were illegitimate. Since, in the eyes of the Catholic Church, Elizabeth was not a legitimate heir, she had no right to be queen, as the bull *Regnans in Excelsis* asserts. From her point of view, the bull therefore looked like an attempt to undermine all of the legal, moral and religious justifications for Elizabeth's rule. Worse, it threatened to include any of her subjects in excommunication if they continued to take their allegiance to her seriously, and if they obeyed her commands. Obedience and allegiance were key concepts in the Tudor theory of government.

16

*Cardinal William Allen, from a portrait at Ushaw College, and
Queen Elizabeth I from British Library Egerton MS 2572*

*The Babington plotters, from 'A Grateful Remembrance
of God's Mercy' by George Carleton, 1630,
and the Durham Martyrs memorial.*

*Boste's capture and trial, from the printed edition of the 1910 play 'The Cost of a Crown' by R.H. Benson*

*Ushaw College today and a detail of the triptych by Geoffrey Webb at Ushaw: Boste is the kneeling figure on the left. Photos by Sean M Smith, © the Trustees of Ushaw College.*

# 3. The Other Queen

An additional source of worry for Elizabeth's Protestant government was the continued existence of a Catholic queen, Mary Queen of Scots, on English soil.

The dangerous political and military situation in Scotland had forced Mary to flee to England in 1568, at the age of twenty-six. Thereafter she had become a prisoner of Queen Elizabeth, and remained so until her death, nearly twenty years later. The Scottish queen experienced a rather comfortable imprisonment, during which she was allowed servants, an income and a degree of communication with the outside world. She was held in a bewildering variety of locations throughout England, including Bolton, Coventry, Chatsworth and Sheffield. She was even allowed to stay at the spa town of Buxton in Derbyshire to take the waters and improve her health.

If Mary had been content with this life, which was comparable to the life of one of the 'prisoner knights' who lived as honoured hostages in the royal courts of Europe in the middle ages, she may have lived well into the seventeenth century, outliving Queen Elizabeth I and perhaps even attending the coronation of her son James as king of England in 1603. But it was not to be. Mary was keen to assert her status as a potential Catholic queen of England in waiting, as a great-granddaughter of King Henry VII, Elizabeth's grandfather.

To some Catholics, Mary Stuart was a stronger heir to the English throne than Elizabeth, because they maintained, as we have seen, that Henry VIII's divorce from Katherine of Aragon was invalid, and that Elizabeth was therefore illegitimate. Great Britain's 'other queen' was also pious, beautiful and accomplished, and nearly ten years younger than her cousin, Elizabeth. In 1566, two years before her English captivity began, she had also given birth to a son, an occasion that caused Elizabeth to utter the melancholy line, 'The queen of Scots is this day lighter of a fair son, and I am but a barren stock'.

Mary was tempted to encourage, or at least not to discourage, various plots designed to remove Elizabeth and place her, Mary, on the English throne. She managed this via what she assumed to be secret communication channels between herself and various conspirators in the British Isles and on the Continent. What she did not realise was the extent to which Sir Francis Walsingham, Elizabeth's spy-master, and others, knew about these plots, the participants in which often included agents of Walsingham who acted as informants and *agents provocateurs*.

The Scottish queen's tendency to become involved in plots led to her being placed in the hands of the Somerset Puritan Sir Amias Paulet, who supervised her captivity at Chartley Castle in Staffordshire from January 1585. Paulet was immune to Mary's considerable charms, and successfully cut off any secret communications she enjoyed with the outside world. Mary was therefore delighted when what she thought was a secret communication, which had been 'hidden' in a beer-barrel, reached her in July 1586. This had been written by one Anthony Babington, who believed himself to be heading up a thriving conspiracy that would lead to the assassination of Elizabeth, the invasion of England from Spain and the eventual coronation of the Scottish queen, presumably as Queen Mary II.

If the Babington plot, as it is called, had succeeded, the catalogue of English kings and queens would not only have included a sixteenth-century Mary II: since Mary's third husband, the Scotsman James Hepburn, Earl of Bothwell, had died insane in a Danish gaol in 1578, Queen Mary would have been free to marry again, so that the list of English monarchs might have included not only Henry VIII, a king who had married six times, but a queen who had had four husbands. In this alternative history scenario, England, Scotland and Wales might have been converted back to Roman Catholicism, ushering in a repetition of aspects of the short reign of Queen Mary I.

But unknown to Mary Stuart, and to Babington and some of the other conspirators, their plot was doomed to failure – indeed it had been designed to fail, since several of the key conspirators were working as double-agents for Walsingham. Every letter Mary had fished out of a beer-barrel had already been opened, deciphered, read and recorded by Walsingham's agents, then carefully re-sealed and put back in the barrel in such a way that it did not look as if anyone had tampered with it. Walsingham even got away with adding a section to a letter of Mary's, that had been sent out via one of the empty beer-barrels. The empty barrels were regularly collected by the brewer who had supplied the beer (with its secret ingredient) in the first place. This doctored letter was passed on to the conspirators, who did not suspect that their 'secret' method of reaching Mary had been compromised in any way.

Meanwhile the brewer, known only by the code-name 'The Honest Man', was making a tidy profit. He was selling his beer, but he was also selling his services to the conspirators, and to the English government. While Mary was congratulating herself about her new line of communication, the only line she was really getting was enough metaphorical rope to hang herself (although in the event she was beheaded and not hanged).

Now John Boste was active on the outer fringes of the Babington conspiracy, serving as a messenger between the conspirators and some Scottish lords who were sympathetic to Mary Stuart. The news he brought to the conspirators, including the Jesuit John Ballard, whom he had known for some time, cannot, however, have been very encouraging. Questioned after his arrest, Ballard confirmed that Boste had brought him news of the distinct lukewarmness of the Scots lords. They wanted support from France, but were not getting it; they could not act alone, and they criticised the English Catholics for their lack of commitment.

Boste's involvement with the Babington conspirators, however slight it was, is important because, even as he was being led to his death in 1594, he denied acting against Queen Elizabeth.

By the time the Babington conspiracy got underway, Boste had been an active Catholic priest in England for five years. He had arrived in 1581, the year after Edmund Campion, and his journey to this high-risk way of life resembled the more famous Campion's progress in many ways. Both were from comparatively humble families, Campion being the son of a London bookseller and Boste the son of a landowner, Nicholas Boste, who lived at Wellying Manor at Dufton in Westmorland (now a village in the modern county of Cumbria). Both men were clever enough to become Oxford fellows, Campion at St John's College and Boste at the more ancient Queen's College, a fourteenth-century foundation.

Like Campion, Boste became a priest of the Protestant Church of England, which they would later both regard as heretical. Boste also served for a while as headmaster of his old school, Appleby Grammar, which still exists.

Boste lost his fellowship of Queen's after 1576 because by this time he had become a Roman Catholic. He had probably been received into that religion at Browne Hall in Suffolk, the house of the leading Catholic, Sir Thomas Cornwallis. Cornwallis had been an important man under the Catholic Queen Mary I: he sat on her council and in her parliaments, and his wife, also called Mary, was a lady of Queen Mary's privy chamber.

When Elizabeth I became queen, Cornwallis lost his grand positions and retired to Browne Hall, but like many known Catholics at the time he suffered as a result of the rising of 1569. He was interrogated, and imprisoned for a year, then freed to confront the difficult questions that faced all the English Catholics of his generation: how could he be regarded as loyal to the queen while maintaining a different religion, and should he avoid prosecution by 'conforming', i.e. attending a Church of England service from time to time? The third question Catholics had to answer was whether they were prepared to risk further trouble by sheltering priests, holding possibly incriminating documents, celebrating the Roman Mass, and encouraging others to convert, or return to, the old religion?

For a while, Sir Thomas did conform, but during Protestant church services he merely sat reading his Catholic books. Although his sons William and Charles continued to conform, Thomas had become a recusant again by 1578, and it seems that his wife and daughters never conformed. Like Anthony Browne, the first Viscount Montagu, with whom Boste was later associated, Cornwallis was so rich, powerful, respected and well-connected that, for his family, the consequences of their recusancy were not as serious as they were for many poorer, more obscure people who, for instance, could not afford to pay the fines imposed on recusants.

By the time Boste arrived on the Continent, ready to study at William Allen's English seminary, the college had been forced to move temporarily from Douai to Rheims in France. This move is recorded in the name usually applied to the magnificent Douay–Rheims Bible, a translation specially created for the use of English Catholics. The Douay–Rheims New Testament, usually called the Rheims New Testament, was published in France in 1582, and was soon appearing in English Catholic houses. John Boste did not live to see the publication of the Douay–Rheims Old Testament, which appeared much later, in 1609-10.

Boste arrived at Rheims in 1580, and returned to England as a fully-fledged Catholic missionary priest in April 1581, landing at Hartlepool on the north-east coast. Like his fellow covert priests, John was forced to go in disguise and have a 'cover' identity, like a modern police officer doing undercover work. At one point, Boste was going around in 'a cloak of rat's colour, a white frieze jerkin laid with blue lace and in a pair of buff leather hose'. A great deal of effort was spent perfecting these false personae, which went much further than just un-priest-like costumes. The younger missionary priest, John Gerard, who returned to England the year after Boste, was so expert at this that his story reminds us of the exploits of the fictional spy, James Bond. Gerard was so successful at projecting the image of a shallow sportsman and gambler that some of his Catholic hosts were astounded when he revealed himself to be the priest whose visit they had been expecting.

Gerard's older contemporary John Boste posed as a 'servant' in the family of the aforementioned Anthony Browne, Viscount Montagu, who like Sir Thomas Cornwallis had been a leading man during the reign of the Catholic Queen Mary I. Mary married Philip, then a Spanish prince, in 1554, and for a time Browne was master of his horse. He became Viscount Montagu at the time of Mary's marriage to Philip at Hampton Court, when his second wife Magdalen was part of the bridal procession. Browne also became a knight of the garter and privy councillor, and served Philip and Mary as an ambassador. Later, Magdalen attended the funerals of both Queen Mary and Mary Queen of Scots.

Like Thomas Cornwallis, Anthony Browne did experience a loss of status after the accession of Elizabeth, but although he was dropped from the privy council, he still did important work for the regime, including sitting on the committee that tried the Queen of Scots. He also worked as an ambassador, despite his outspoken defences of Catholicism in the House of Lords. Although he was a well-known Catholic, and frequently under suspicion, he was given the honour of entertaining Elizabeth for six days at one of his homes, Cowdray Park in Sussex, in the summer of 1591.

Browne's second wife Magdalen was so active in sheltering priests and hosting masses at one of the family's other houses, Battle Abbey in Sussex, that her neighbours started referring to the place as Little Rome. Her confessor Richard Smith, who had studied and taught at Douai and in Spain, wrote an admiring biography of her that was published in France in 1627.

# 4. The Fugitive

While John Boste could number the Cornwallis and Browne families among his contacts in the south of England, his friends in the north included the Neville family, and the Hyltons of his home county of Westmorland; said to be descended from the Hyltons of Hylton Castle near Sunderland.

It was a strategy of the fugitive priests of the time to seek help from wealthy Catholic families: these people could support them financially, provide them with fake roles as covers in their sometimes large households, give them food, shelter and transport, arrange for their secure communication with the outside world, and provide them with appropriate spaces where they could celebrate masses and other religious services. Sometimes as many as one hundred and twenty people would gather for such services at Battle Abbey during the time of Magdalen Browne, and local Catholics could travel to such houses to make their confession.

In Magdalen's houses, it might sometimes have been possible for Catholics to imagine that Queen Mary I was still alive, and England still a Catholic country. Despite occasional searches of her properties, and the capture of one of the priests she harboured, Magdalen continued to shelter them: their number even included the great-grandchild of the martyr Thomas More.

Lady Magdalen also built a fine chapel in her house at Battle, complete with a stone altar at the top of some steps, and altar-rails: these features immediately identified the chapel as a Catholic place of worship.

Since families like the Brownes often had several homes, priests disguised as servants could travel between them with members of the family, and accompany aristocrats on their visits to family and friends elsewhere.

Many of the aristocratic shelterers of priests could afford to have one or more priest-holes installed in their houses: sometimes these hiding-places were so ingenious that it would not be a surprise to learn, at some point in the near future, that one had been re-discovered after having been forgotten for over four hundred years. Some of these priest-holes were installed by the remarkable Jesuit, Nicholas Owen, who was tortured to death under King James I and, like John Boste, canonised in 1970.

As we have seen, in the case of the Cornwallis family, and especially the Sussex Brownes, even outspoken members of aristocratic recusant households could avoid harassment simply because they were so wealthy, powerful and respected. In the case of Anthony Browne, it would seem that his talent as an ambassador and negotiator meant that Elizabeth's government simply had to employ him in important positions, and Elizabeth's own stay at Cowdray Park suggests that she personally liked the family, though Anthony had openly opposed her religious policies on several occasions.

Especially where the servants in these households were all Catholics themselves, they might be less liable to be bribed or intimidated into betraying the covert priest or priests, and the presence of so many Catholics in these 'Little Romes' would allow the priest to remember what he was, and what he was doing in England.

As well as confinement for long periods in priest-holes, the constant danger of a government raid, and the strain of maintaining a false identity, there must have been serious temptations for covert priests like Boste as they lived concealed lives in the recusant houses of the time. Since homes were very much female preserves in those days, priests, who had spent years in the overwhelmingly male atmosphere of the Continental seminaries, would suddenly find themselves in the care of a woman, and having regular contact with other women, whether they were servants of the house, members of the family, visitors, or people attending secret services or looking for spiritual counsel.

John Boste and his comrades no doubt advised those who sought their advice about how they should tackle the serious problems that beset them as adherents of the old religion in what was becoming a very Protestant country. What if they were Catholic, but their husband, children or other relatives were not? Should they continue to conceal their Catholicism? How were they to pay their fines for recusancy, and cope with the other punitive measures the government had dreamed up? Should they let their son go abroad and train as a priest?

In a letter probably sent in 1584 to Andrew, a member of the aforementioned Hylton family, Boste took an uncompromising line on the tricky subject of Catholics attending Church of England services merely to avoid the label of 'recusant' and all the inconveniences that brought with it. A single page of this letter to Hylton, who it seems was attending some Church of England services, still exists, and in it Boste accuses Christians like Andrew of being disobedient 'bastards', who strive against God, and are not His true children. They are dissemblers, sowing discord and division, and deserving God's curse. Boste claims that such people are disapproved of by St Paul and the doctors of the church, meaning learned Christians of the past such as the Venerable Bede, whose remains lie in Durham Cathedral, just a short walk from the place outside Durham where Boste was martyred.

In his letter, Boste claims that the Protestant Church lacks antiquity and that it cannot, like the Catholic Church, claim to be a church descended from St Peter. He also claims that the 'lewd' new church has no martyrs to boast of. This assertion seems odd in the English context, since Protestant martyrs had been made during the reign of Queen Mary, and there were other Protestant martyrs both in the British Isles and elsewhere. No doubt Boste felt that, as from his point of view they were in error theologically, these were not really martyrs at all.

In 1584, the same year Boste may have sent his letter to Andrew Hylton, William of Orange, the Dutch Protestant leader, was assassinated at Delft. Some of the guilt for this assassination had to attach to Philip II, the king of Spain, as he had declared William an outlaw and offered a huge reward for anyone who managed to kill him. William's death gave the Protestant authorities in England yet another reason to fear the power of Spain's Catholic empire.

Four years after William's assassination and Boste's letter to Andrew Hylton, seven years after Boste returned to England as a missionary, and three years into the late sixteenth-century war between England and Spain, England's coasts were threatened by the Spanish Armada. The launch of this huge fleet of one hundred and thirty ships was supposed to be the first move in a planned conquest of Protestant England by Catholic Spain, which would see Queen Elizabeth deposed.

Among those who believed that the Spanish invasion would succeed was Cardinal William Allen, the mastermind of the Douai College, which had been forced to move to Rheims when Boste trained there. Not for the first time, Allen began to plan the reconversion of England to the old religion, a process in which he saw himself playing an important part. In 1583, before a previous planned invasion, Allen had been told that he would be the papal legate to England, and also the Bishop of Durham, should the scheme succeed. Before the failure of the Armada in 1588, the cardinal planned to combine the roles of Archbishop of Canterbury and Lord Chancellor. Eager to take up his new positions, he even tried to travel to the Netherlands so as to be ready to cross over to England quickly when he was called for.

Many English Protestants regarded the defeat of the Armada, which was partly due to bad weather, as proof that God was, if not an Englishman, then definitely on the side of Elizabeth's regime. Catholic Spain was confirmed once again as a major threat, and the fact that the Armada had been assembled at all suggested that Catholic Europe was out to get Protestant England. Wanted men before, Boste, his comrades and those who aided them now had even more reason to look over their shoulders.

There is no doubt that the authorities were out to get Boste, not just because of his peripheral involvement in the Babington plot but also because he was known to be an effective, inspiring, hard-working priest whose mere presence on what we might call the 'underground railroad' of recusant England did wonders for the morale and resolve of his widely-scattered flock. The fact that he had escaped arrest since 1581 made him an even more sought-after prize, and also an engrossing puzzle for the authorities.

The man ultimately charged with Boste's apprehension was Henry Hastings, Earl of Huntingdon. A high-born Puritan who was evidently regarded as a safe pair of hands by Queen Elizabeth, Huntingdon had been put in charge of the captive Queen of Scots at the time of the rising in 1569, and by the time Boste returned to England in 1582, he had held the leading position of President of the Council of the North for a decade. As Elizabeth's viceroy in Yorkshire, Durham, Northumberland, Cumberland and Westmorland, Huntingdon not only hunted Catholics and promoted Protestantism – he had also been responsible for defending a long stretch of England's North Sea coastline as the Armada sailed past it in 1588.

The capture of Boste at Waterhouses near Durham in September 1593 was considered so important that the queen was immediately informed, and her delight at the news was conveyed to Huntingdon in a letter from William Cecil, Lord Burghley, Elizabeth's Secretary of State. In October Huntingdon replied:

I pray God her majesty may at the last have all the principals of his faction and society, if the whole rabble of them cannot be gotten, or driven out of the land; which were to be wished, for none do more impeach the happy government of her majesty, than these wicked seminaries and Jesuits do, who under the pretence of holiness, plant chiefly treason, and treacherous conceits against her majesty in the hearts of those subjects, with whom they do prevail.

Later in the same letter, Huntingdon cautiously requests that London should send a message to those 'which serve abroad in the realm' warning them that it is their job to hunt down 'such guests' and that 'winking and slack dealing', i.e. turning a blind eye and letting things slip, are not acceptable. In another letter to Burghley, Tobie Mathew, then Dean of Durham, complained about 'intercessions and mediations from above' which had hampered the efforts of the priest-hunters to the 'great inconvenience' of both 'religion and realm'.

In his letter to Burghley, Huntingdon also complained that he has 'been often and greatly abused by those which I have trusted for the taking of him [Boste]', a reference, perhaps, to his distaste at having to deal with such slimy characters as Francis Egglesfield, the spy who betrayed Boste.

A former Catholic, Egglesfield would pose as one of the faithful and ingratiate himself with the members of recusant households. This he did at the Waterhouse, now long gone, the home of the Catholic Claxton family, which stood by Brancepeth Castle near Durham, which is still standing. In the wake of the 1569 rising, the castle had been taken away from the powerful Catholic Neville family, and turned into a prison for recusants and Catholic priests who had had the bad luck to be captured.

A number of local Catholics, including Lady Margaret Neville, had gathered at the Waterhouse on the tenth of September 1593. John Boste conducted a Mass there, and as the congregation left the building Francis Egglesfield asked Father Boste for a blessing. Boste agreed, not realising that this would be the signal for the soldiers concealed in the woods around the house to help them identify Boste, their quarry. The soldiers revealed themselves, and Boste rushed off into the house. A search was rapidly conducted, but the priest, who had been betrayed much as Jesus had been betrayed by Judas, could not be found. The modern Judas knew, however, where he was. Egglesfield commanded the soldiers to break through a wall above a fire-place, where Boste was at last found, in the Waterhouse priest-hole.

Soon Boste and Lady Margaret were locked up in the nearby Brancepeth Castle.

## 5. An Act of Faith

The first examination of John Boste, shortly after his capture in September 1593, was important enough to be attended by Huntingdon, by Tobie Mathew, the aforementioned Dean of Durham, and by Sir William Bowes, another member of the Council of the North.

The upshot of the examination, held at Durham, was a confession signed by both Boste and Huntingdon in which the former admitted to breaking the law by leaving England without permission, to train as a priest at Rheims. He said he was one of twenty-five priests sent back to England from Rheims, of whom Ballard, the Babington plotter, was one. Boste also admitted that he had visited various people in Scotland, but had not been in that country for five years: and he had never crossed the sea to the Continent or anywhere else since his arrival at Hartlepool in 1581. During 1593 he had concentrated his efforts on Yorkshire, Durham and Northumberland, and had spent whole months at a time in Yorkshire.

Striking a note of defiance, Boste, who confirmed that he was indeed the Englishman John Boste who had been born at Dufton in Westmorland, admitted that he had said Mass in various places, but he would not say where and he could not say how many times. In the words of his signed confession, 'if he said not every day a Mass, it was against his will'.

One Anthony Atkinson, apparently a spy of the same stamp as Boste's personal Judas, Francis Egglesfield, was present when Boste was taken, and also questioned him. He managed to get *some* information out of him, but remarked in a letter that 'Boste makes it a [matter of] conscience not to accuse no man in matters that may concern life'. Atkinson hoped, however, to be able to get more out of the prisoner 'if he be used in courteous manner and not too hardly punished'. He also expected more information about Boste from more talkative prisoners then in custody.

Boste having not revealed anything much of value that his captors did not already know, he was quickly shipped off to the Tower of London, to be tortured by, among others, Elizabeth's torturer-in-chief, Richard Topcliffe. There he was so severely racked that he was never able to stand up straight again without the aid of a staff, and 'when he sat on his knees (as for the most part he ever was) he was all in a heap, as if he had been all in pieces'.

Topcliffe reported to Sir John Puckering, Lord Keeper of the Privy Seal and one-time Speaker of the House of Commons, that Boste was 'a resolute traitor'. The defiance he had shown at Durham had re-surfaced under questioning in London, when a lesser man would have revealed everything he knew about the recusant network in England, naming many names. At an earlier examination, before Topcliffe got him into the Tower, Boste said that he wished there were twenty priests 'for every one Popish priest in England', and stated that he regretted not having converted twenty people to Catholicism for every one he did convert. Asked where his loyalties lay, Boste answered that he had to obey the pope, but that if the pope himself sent an army against England, then he, Boste, would fight on the English side. This was his answer to a question that was routinely put to recusants and captured priests, to test their fidelity to the crown.

Our most detailed eye-witness account of Boste's trial and execution in Durham comes from a letter written by one Christopher Robinson, who was himself martyred at Carlisle shortly after. Christopher rode all the way from Boste's home county of Westmorland, setting out on Tuesday the twenty-third of July 1594 'that I should on the morrow after see at Durham that martyr die'.

Robinson tells us that Boste was tried together with a fellow-priest called John Ingram, and a Catholic layman, George Swallowfield, who had once been a minister of the Church of England. Swallowfield, suddenly seized with terror at the thought of being hanged, drawn and quartered, declared during the trial that he would abandon his Catholicism, attend a Church of England service, and 'acknowledge the queen to be supreme in spiritual matters'. Something like this climb-down had been used by Lady Margaret Neville, who was taken with Boste at the Waterhouse. In a letter to the queen, she claimed that she had fallen in with the Catholics because of the poverty of her family that had followed on from the revolt of 1569. Thanks to the 'subtlety' of the Catholics, she was 'allured from mine obedience and loyalty, to their superstition and errors'. Margaret's letter proved to be enough to save her neck, but she later reverted to Catholicism again.

At their trial at Durham, Ingram and Boste succeeded in steadying Swallowfield's resolve, telling him to 'profess that faith with your mouth, which we know you believe with your heart'. Swallowfield followed their advice, and cried out, 'I am resolved! I am resolved'.

The judge at the trial, where Lord President Huntingdon was also present, was Sir Francis Beaumont, father of the playwright, also called Francis. Sir Francis the judge sentenced other Catholics to death, including the Jesuit martyr Henry Walpole, who died at York in 1595; but Beaumont and his family had a reputation as Catholic sympathisers. Sir Francis seldom attended Church of England services, his wife corresponded with known recusants, and his mother may have harboured Edmund Campion in 1581.

After the jury's verdict had been heard, and before the prisoners received the terrible sentence of hanging, drawing and quartering, Beaumont favoured Boste, Ingram and Swallowfield with his thoughts on why they should be condemned. 'You have behaved yourselves as undutiful and naughty subjects,' he said, 'who have gone about by all means possible to withdraw from her majesty's subjects their good affection, obedience and loyalty which faithful and loyal subjects ought in conscience to give to their sovereign'.

Now speaking *about* the prisoners instead of *to* them, Beaumont posed two rhetorical questions which he then answered himself:

And how do they steal into their bosoms, and withdraw their minds? They come into this realm with the pope's bulls forsooth and tell the people they are not bound any more to be subject to her highness. And why? Because Pius or Sixtus Quintus hath excommunicated our queen long ago and deprived her, as you say, of all power of regiment [rule] whatsoever; nay, and hath commanded, say you, all her subjects to give no more obedience unto her under pain of excommunication.

Moving on to events far away which had no direct relevance to the case at hand, Beaumont claimed that:

In Spain there is one Parsons who stirreth up the king to make war against her highness and carrieth away that good mind, which otherwise he would bear unto her. And in Italy Cardinal Allen incenseth the pope daily to address his forces and to exhaust the Church treasures for the subversion of our country, pulling her out of her throne to the utter ruin of us all.

We have already met Cardinal Allen, the mastermind behind the English College at Douai: 'one Parsons' was in fact Robert Persons, an influential English Jesuit who was in England as a Catholic missionary in 1580 and 1581, and later became rector of the English College at Rome.

Shifting from developments overseas back into remote British history, Boste's judge related a story of King Lucius, a saintly second-century king of the Britons who is supposed to have written to the Bishop of Rome, asking him to, in effect, write laws for the British. The bishop, said Beaumont, 'being a very good man', would not 'usurp the name of pope', and wrote back to Lucius saying that he, Lucius, should use the Bible and the advice of his local bishops to write his own laws. 'By which epistle it is manifest' said the judge, 'that the Bishop of Rome gave then that authority to the Bishops of England which now you give to the pope'. Not

36

surprisingly, Beaumont refused to debate this whimsical argument with the prisoners, 'for ye be learned'.

Beaumont concluded his remarks with his sentence:

For these your unnatural proceedings against your prince, and horrible treasons against your country, I am now to proceed in judgement against you, which is this. You shall be carried to the place from whence you came, and from thence you shall be carried either upon a sled, or upon a hurdle unto the place of execution: there you shall be hanged by the necks. Presently you shall be cut down, and your members shall be cut from you and cast into the fire even in your own sight, your bowels shall be pulled out of your bodies and cast likewise into the fire, your heads shall be cut off, your bodies shall be quartered and the parts of your bodies shall be disposed as officers shall see occasion.

Christopher Robinson's account of Boste's martyrdom at Dryburn outside Durham on the twenty-fourth of July 1594 is truly heart-breaking. A large number of people, including many 'country gentlewomen' turned out to watch. Although it seems that the sheriff who was in charge of the proceedings tried to hang Boste long enough for him to be dead when the hangman began to cut him up, the martyr revived and even spoke as the grisly business proceeded. Among other words spoken by him on the gallows were his oath that he 'never went about to hurt' Queen Elizabeth, and that he hoped his blood 'may be in satisfaction for her sins'. For a short time, Boste's head was exhibited on a pole on Framwellgate Bridge in Durham, but this was soon stolen away by one of the faithful. Ingram and Swallowfield were later martyred, at Gateshead and Darlington respectively.

As we know, Boste never left Great Britain after his arrival at Hartlepool in April 1581. When he was studying for the priesthood, the English College at Douai had been forced to relocate temporarily to Rheims in France. If Boste had fled England and returned to his *Alma Mater* in 1593, he would have found the college back in its old home of Douai. It continued there until 1795, and in 1808 opened its doors again as St Cuthbert's College, just a few miles to the west of Durham. Now known as Ushaw College, John Boste is commemorated there in a large triptych painting by Geoffrey Webb that shows a selection of Catholic martyrs, and also one of the Douai buildings, and the Tower of London. As the painting reminds us, Boste was only one of many seminary priests who perished in England during the reign of the first Elizabeth. Of the four hundred and seventy-one priests known to have been active in England during her reign, no less than one hundred and thirty-three were either executed or died in prison – nearly thirty percent.

The priests who perished under Elizabeth make up rather less than half of all the Catholics who died for their beliefs in England in the sixteenth and seventeenth centuries. Of these, twenty-six are thought to have had links to Durham, where Boste was active and where he was martyred. One was the aforementioned Thomas Plumtree, who celebrated Mass in Durham Cathedral during the rebellion of 1569: Thomas was executed in the Durham Market Place in 1570, thus becoming the first Catholic priest to be martyred under Elizabeth I.

Edmund Duke, Richard Hill, Richard Holiday and John Hogg were missionary priests who were trained on the Continent like Boste and returned to England rather later than he did – in 1590. Unfortunately they were soon captured and executed at Dryburn outside Durham less than a year after their arrival. Later, but just a few months before Boste's execution, a layman called John Speed, who had assisted Boste in his travels, was also executed at Durham.

Other Durham martyrs include Thomas Palaser, a priest trained at Rheims, who was arrested at Ravensworth near Lamesley in County Durham. Two more martyrs; John Norton, who owned the house at Ravensworth, and John Talbot, were taken with Palaser, as was Norton's wife: she escaped execution because she was thought to be pregnant. The three men are sometimes known as the Lamesley Martyrs, and they were all executed at Durham on the ninth of August 1600.

John Ingram, who was tried at Durham with Boste and executed at Gateshead, was born in 1565, the year after Shakespeare, and like the playwright was also a Warwickshire man. Like Boste, he also studied at Oxford, and was tortured in the Tower of London.

In 1970 John Boste became one of the Forty Martyrs of England and Wales canonised by Pope Paul VI. The Forty include a number of saints we have already met in this book – Margaret Clitherow, Edmund Campion, Nicholas Owen (the builder of priest-holes) and Cuthbert Mayne, the first of the Catholic priests trained abroad to be executed, in 1577 (Thomas Plumtree was not trained on the Continent).

Other interesting saints among the Forty include Robert Southwell, arrested the year before Boste and also tortured by Topcliffe, but executed at Tyburn in London, and not Dryburn outside Durham. Southwell was an important poet and prose-writer, as well as a Jesuit priest, and his work is said to have influenced a number of later writers, including Shakespeare and George Herbert. Southwell was a companion of John Gerard, the covert priest whose exploits are reminiscent of those of James Bond. Gerard was never martyred, and even managed to escape from the Tower of London. He died in Rome in 1637, at the age of seventy-three.

In 1974, four years after he became a saint, the John Boste Catholic primary school was founded in nearby Washington, Tyne and Wear.

Some of the martyrs mentioned above are included under the name the Durham Martyrs, to whose memory there is now a monument outside Durham City, near where Boste and some of the others were martyred. Nearby there is also a street, in a new housing estate, called Boste Crescent. In 2013 the local Catholic Church in Durham decided to merge two of its parishes to create the Durham Martyrs parish. The parish has close links with St Leonard's Roman Catholic school outside Durham, somewhere on the site of which John Boste and some of the others were executed, during the golden age of the first Elizabeth.

# Select Bibliography

Beaumont, Edward T: *The Beaumonts in History*, 1929

Benson, Robert Hugh: *The Cost of a Crown*, Longmans, 1910

Burgess, Anthony: *Shakespeare*, Vintage, 1996

Campbell, W.J.: *Ushaw College 1808-2008, a Celebration*, St Cuthbert's Society, 2008

Cross, Claire: *The Puritan Earl*, Macmillan, 1966

Dufferwiel, Martin: *Durham: Over 1,000 Years of History and Legend*, Mainstream, 2004

Emery, Norman: *Saint John Boste and the Waterhouse*, Norman Emery, 1982

Haile, Martin: *An Elizabethan Cardinal*, Pitman, 1914

Hasler, P.W.(ed.): *The History of Parliament: The House of Commons*, 1558-1603, TSO, 1981

Hogge, Alice: *God's Secret Agents*, Harper, 2009

Kelly, James E.: *Treasures of Ushaw College*, Scala, 2015

Milburn, David: *A History of Ushaw College*, Ushaw College, 1964

Myerscough, John A: *The Martyrs of Durham and the North-East*, Burns, 1956

Neale, J. E.: *Queen Elizabeth I*, Penguin, 1960

Pollen, John Hungerford: *Unpublished Documents Relating to the English Martyrs, Volume I*, Catholic Record Society, 1908

Sharp, Cuthbert: *Memorials of the Rebellion of 1569*, John Bowyer Nichols, 1840

Southern, A.C.: *An Elizabethan Recusant House*, Sands & Co., 1954

Southwell, Robert: *The Complete Works of Robert Southwell*, Hansebooks, 2017

St John Boste Celebrations Committee: *St John Boste and the Continuity of Catholicism in the Deerness Valley*, Newhouse Church, 1993

Surtees, Conyers: *The History of the Castle of Brancepeth*, 1920

Surtees, Conyers: *The History of the Parish of Brancepeth*, 1930

Waugh, Evelyn: *Edmund Campion*, Longmans, 1961

Website of Ushaw College: www.ushaw.org

For free downloads and more from the Langley Press, please visit our website at: http://tinyurl.com/lpdirect